AUDACIOUS AUTHENTICITY

A KICK-ASS PATH TO BEING REAL
IN A FAKE-ASS WORLD

ROBIN BROWN-WOOD

Li'l Liva
Publishing

AUDACIOUS AUTHENTICITY
A Kick-Ass Path to Being Real in a Fake-Ass World
published by Li'l Liva Publishing
copyright © 2021 Robin Brown-Wood

Meraki Mindset is a trademark of Robin Brown-Wood.

ISBN (print):   978-1-7374240-0-0
ISBN (eBook):   978-1-7374240-1-7

Cover Design and Illustrations
Val Stilwell/GrowthCollab.com
Val@GrowthCollab.com

Editing, Interior Book Design & Production
Eva Long/Long On Books
eva@longonbooks.com

Author's Photo
Chea LaTourette
www.cheastudio.com

Printed in the United States of America

This book is dedicated to my parents
who gave me life-affirming values:
to my husband who always
makes being an Authentic look so easy;
and to my carefully chosen close circle of friends
who stay in my circle by keeping it real.

To Sharie –

Keep it 100...

Robin

CONTENTS

AUTHOR'S NOTE

An Authentic is about presence, living in the moment with conviction and confidence and staying true to yourself. ~ Christopher D. Connors

LET ME CLARIFY RIGHT OFF THE bat that I am in no way a licensed anything. I hold a formal degree in psychology (a minor to my major which was physical education). My fascination with the human brain began as early as grade school and somewhere along the way, I decided to become a student of human behavior. I believed that there was no better place to begin than by studying my own. Almost immediately I saw that my own behavior was greatly affected by others'. I've gone through enough therapy, self-help, and reading material to arrive at a point in my life to declare myself an Authentic—living true to who I am. This is why I wrote this book. I've always felt I had a message to share with others who might be daring, dreaming, or even fearing being an Authentic themselves but not sure of the why or how to get there. A business colleague fanned this flame when she suggested I write a book.

"Sure," I said, "why not?" Not one to back down from an opportunity to be challenged and thus grow, I decided to go for it.

This book is structured so that it allows you to gain knowledge, assess the knowledge, and apply the knowledge. I hope you will engage with this book from the front cover to the last page. There are no right or wrong answers to the questions asked at the end of each chapter; they are meant to help you discover layers of your personality yet uncovered.

Bend the pages to earmark something you want to remember; write in the book, write outside of the book, share this book with those who care enough to be on an authentic path, and/or create a book club discussion about this book.

You'll also find a coloring assignment! Allow yourself to abandon any fears or restricting thoughts as you take colored pens, pencils or crayons to the mandalas. Color these with abandon, especially if that means coloring outside of the lines.

Lastly, let the inspirational quotes become daily mantras for you as you navigate through this thing called Life. Resolve to make choices in keeping with your desire to be on your most authentic path and take the biggest bites ever to support that goal.

I hope that what follows will open up pathways for you to question and clarify your own authenticity and create a wonderful path for you to follow to become an Authentic. These are observations and experiences from my own journey and many scholarly professionals. I wish for you much success on your journey. ~

~BEING AN AUTHENTIC
AND ITS INTRINSIC VALUES
Fake is the New Real

Only the truth of who you are, if realized, will set you free.

~ Eckhart Tolle

C AN YOU TELL THE DIFFERENCE BETWEEN turkey bacon and regular bacon? Would you know the difference between a fake Gucci and a real one? Can you identify real wood from plastic wood? If you could afford it, would you pay top dollar for a fake product when you could own the real one? Can you tell when someone is being an Authentic with you or whether they're fake as a million-dollar bill? Can you tell when you're being real and when you're not?

3

Why is being an Authentic so important? Why do we need to be "genuine" or "true"? What is your reaction when confronted with these fakes? Irritation? Doubt in the quality? No emotional connection? When faced with real bacon or a Gucci or real wood, there's a level of trust and an emotional connection because we know the real thing merits honesty, quality, and truth. These are the same qualities we look for in other people and more importantly, hope we have these same qualities ourselves.

Over the years, in my many professions that were all public service related, I have interacted with many people who lacked personal authenticity. I equate this kind of fakeness to "being in the closet" or walking around with a plastic bag over one's head. Some people want so badly to fit in and be accepted that they create a manufactured persona that keeps them from being rejected or ostracized by the people with whom they surround themselves. Their created persona is not who they really are but their need is so great to fit in that they're willing to sacrifice important things like money, relationships, and even their integrity for validation and to fit in. In this process of creating their persona, they're smothering their natural personality and creating a host of other health, mental, and even spiritual issues that can negatively manifest other challenges.

How does being inauthentic impact the inner self—the *true* self? People may not be aware that not living authentically can also impact their bodies. Lack of quality sleep, indigestion, ulcers, high blood pressure, general fatigue, and a host of other physical ailments can be signs of someone who is living a less than an Authentic life. Spiritually, our happiness may slowly erode over time leaving us feeling empty and lost. Fake personas based on negative self-images wrapped in the expectations of others is enough to make anyone crazy and exhausted! The lack of authenticity can create invisible gaps in relationships we have with others and ourselves.

In their recorded lectures together on "Living Beyond Miracles," Deepak Chopra and Dr. Wayne Dyer, two of my favorite motivational speakers, spoke about self-realization and spiritual fulfillment. I had an "aha" moment listening to Dr. Dyer talk about his family life growing up. He'd always been the odd one out in his family, always marching to the beat of his own drum. His family continually chastised him for not being closer emotionally and for years he allowed their opinions to bother him until one day he made a discovery and a declaration: "From this point on, I'm living my life independent of the good opinion of others," declared Dr. Dyer.

I know I had to rewind it several times after hearing it because it was such a *powerful* statement! I immediately adopted it as my mantra and in doing so I felt this weight lift off of my body, like someone had lifted a hundred-pound barbell off my shoulders. Incredible, because you see, when you decide that no one's opinion of you matters but *your* own, it frees you up to be your *most* authentic self and to make choices aligned with who you really are. I have *never* looked back since that day of enlightenment and I'm suggesting that you, too, might want to look at whether you're living your life for others or for yourself. We only have this one life and wouldn't you have a much richer life if it were filled with truth and authenticity than living your life for someone else?

Let Wayne Dyer's declaration be yours: "From this point on, I'm living my life independent of the good opinion of others." Read this again and again and again. ~

FOOD for THOUGHT:
Who are the people in your life or who you follow
in politics, science, entertainment, education,
that you believe are Authentics?"

_____

_____

_____

_____

_____

_____

_____

_____

_____

_____

_____

_____

_____

_____

_____

_____

_____

_____

_____

RECOGNIZING AN AUTHENTIC

Sherlock Holmes at Your Service

You'll never know who you are unless you shed who you pretend to be.
~ Vironika Tugaleva

HOW DO WE RECOGNIZE AUTHENTICITY IN ourselves? How do we recognize it in others? Here are some easily recognized behavioral signs you can look for to determine authenticity in yourself and in others:

More Is Better?

Do you validate your existence by how many material things you possess? Does having the biggest, fastest, most expensive "thing" make you happy? An Authentic knows that material things are empty and ephemeral—the joy in having them is short-lived. One firey match can take it all away and what you are left with is...yourself.

Life Is a Smorgasbord

An Authentic lives for life experiences and the richness life provides. Doing, being, and discovering far outweigh the emptiness of just "plodding" through life.

I Don't Chew My Cabbage Twice

An Authentic has no problem stating their true thoughts and feelings. They say what they mean and mean what they say without fear of repercussion.

From Your Lips to My Ears

Listening to others without external distractions is another way to spot an Authentic. They genuinely care about what the other is saying and are fully engaged in the conversation.

A Club of One

Fitting into a group isn't important to an Authentic if it means sacrificing their authenticity. Authentics realize that trying to please others is futile.

Health Is Wealth

An Authentic has a healthy level of self-esteem and realizes their own value and self-worth. They take care of themselves first because they know that in doing so, they then have the capacity to take care of others.

Giving Is Receiving

Altruistic generosity is a core value to an Authentic. They give of their abundance—time, material, fiscal, and spiritual—because they genuinely love helping others without the expectations of getting anything in return. They understand that the laws of the Universe work their karmic magic and that helping others helps them as well.

Do "You"

An Authentic embraces their uniqueness. They revel in their own singularity and encourage others to do the same.

Life Is About Choices

An Authentic is mature and realistic enough to take responsibility for their own actions. They don't shift the responsibility to external forces when certain outcomes aren't favorable. They are willing to say "I'm sorry" and mean it with the utmost sincerity. They know that wherever they are in their life is a result of choices they've made throughout their life.

To Err Is Human

Acknowledging and accepting one's faults exemplifies an Authentic. They realize that they are human and that perfection is a false goal to attain. Authentic people realize that others also have faults and, with a nonjudgmental attitude, understand that everyone has their own life story to live.

North Is This Way

Connection to their inner guide or spiritual source quiets the constant inner and outer chatter and is another characteristic of an Authentic. They learn to trust their inner voice (a.k.a. gut instinct) based on an intense faith that it will never steer them down the wrong path. A course of action is taken with supreme confidence; no external validation is necessary.

Where do you see yourself on this list? How would you evaluate yourself as an Authentic? What areas in your life do you want to work on? Who in your circle exhibits one, some, or all of these traits? In our daily comings and goings, we all encounter people who most certainly possess levels of inauthenticity. How do you handle such encounters? Do you have an agreement with your current "tribe" that "I won't hold you to your highest self if you don't hold me to mine?"

The process of being an Authentic is an ongoing process, not short-lived or temporary. In fact, try approaching it with the attitude of excitement—you're going on a journey of a lifetime. This becomes a process of discovering layers about yourself that you didn't know were there so that you can share the real you with the rest of us. What a heady thought! Your attitude determines your aptitude. There's no time like the present to get going. Enjoy the journey! ~

FOOD for THOUGHT:

Have you had to distance yourself from a family member or close friend who was inauthentic? How did that act make you feel? Were you able to channel those feelings into a positive direction or a destructive one?

_____

_____

_____

_____

_____

_____

_____

ASSESSING YOUR OWN AUTHENTICITY

Mirror, Mirror on the Wall

We have to dare to be ourselves, however frightening or strange that self may prove to be.
~ May Sarton

IN THE PREVIOUS CHAPTER I SHARED SOME intrinsic qualities of an authentic personality and encouraged you to start the process of revealing your authentic self. It can be a very exciting process if approached with the right mentality.

There are some things I want to bring to your attention about the process, having gone through it myself (and frankly, still am). Remember, becoming an Authentic takes time; there are no deadlines or "quick fixes" to achieving it. The goal of becoming an Authentic becomes as ingrained into your daily living as does brushing your teeth. Once you determine authenticity as your goal, you consciously make daily choices that allow you to stay on your path.

Check Your Baggage

There will be pain, the degree of which will be different for each person. It depends on how "hidden" you are, and I don't mean that in a pejorative sense. Everyone has emotional baggage from their past and the amount or type will determine how much pain you'll go through to unload. Some baggage is so intensely damaging that help from an external source, such as a therapist or even medical intervention, may be necessary as you embark on your journey. Seeking such help will be well worth it.

Risk Being Vulnerable

A person who truly wants to become an Authentic must be willing to be vulnerable. Read that again because this is a big challenge for a lot of people to handle. Being vulnerable in our society can be seen as being "weak," "needy" or "incompetent." Banish this idea! What separates the authentic person from all others is the willingness to set aside their pride and ego and ask for help.

Take Inventory

As you're assessing the areas you feel need work, you must be *brutal* in your assessment. This is not the time to sugarcoat your self-evaluation. Your goal is Truth and "the truth shall set you free." Look in the mirror—who looks back at you? Be honest!

Kick Fear to the Curb

Lastly, let go of any fear you may have along the way. This is another big challenge for people, and in my humble opinion, has killed more goals and souls than heart disease and cancer combined. I've heard so many people over the years talk themselves out of doing or being something because of fear—fear of success, fear of failure, fear of falling down, fear of "catching fire." Repeat after me: "Life is too short and one day I will not be here. I will not let fear keep me from living my most authentic life."

Let these tips inspire you to start your journey. The truth is on the other side of all of your work and I promise, you will be rewarded. ~

FOOD for THOUGHT:

What challenges do you face in your attempt to honestly assess yourself? Are you filtering your answers to meet other's standards or out of fear of finding answers? Reflect on where you are and where you want to go. Write down some initial steps you can take to make the changes necessary to move forward.

_____

_____

_____

_____

_____

_____

_____

_____

_____

LEARNING TO BECOME AN AUTHENTIC
What Doesn't Kill You Makes You Stronger

The privilege of a lifetime is to become who you truly are.

~ Carl Gustav Jung

Authenticity vs. Social Media

OKAY, LET'S GET STARTED ON BECOMING you doing You. I am going to piss off a lot of people with what I'm about to say, but remember my motto: "I live my life independent of the good opinion of others." So here goes...*get off social media*! I know, I know you're thinking, "Girl be bat-shit crazy!! How will I ever survive without my FB, IG, Twitter, Tik Tok, whatever...My legion of 'fans' won't know what I'm doing 24/7 and I won't know what they're doing!"

Let's be honest. Unless you have a business or service to promote, there is no real reason anyone needs to be on social media. The "me" promotions are just that: "look at me," "love me," "like me," and "want to be me." You know how it goes; you're online just checking out your posts and the responses and the next thing you know, hours have passed with you going down all kinds of rabbit holes you had no intention of exploring. We live our lives creating the next photo opportunity that we can post so we can garner more followers or "likes," and for what? To have our egos stroked by others? And who are these people doing the stroking? People we know but most that we don't. We convince ourselves that their opinions matter so much that our very existence relies on them. We lose sight of who we are, trying to mold ourselves into an image created by the feedback and perceptions both good and bad. We have a good day when social media comments to our posts are positive; we have a bad day when comments are critical.

Our desire to out-live, out-shine, out-follow others on these sites creates little monsters of us—misrepresenting our reality so we look like we're livin' large to the envy of all others. Or maybe you weren't misrepresenting but actually sharing your truth, but for what? Who cares and why? People who are absorbed in the lives of others probably have no lives of their own or are working to escape from their own reality. What's that you say? "How will I keep up with family—parents, kids, grandparents...?" Please! Have we forgotten how to use a phone? Or here's an old-school way—write them!

There's no need to send me any angry comments about these "revolutionary" ideas. I'm not buying any excuses or explanations I hear justifying the need to spend so much of our waking hours on social media.

Fess up: Is any part of this you? I'll confess that this was me for a while until I decided enough was enough. When I noticed I was spending too much time focusing on getting the "likes" instead of creating an even richer life by living, I ceased all social media contact. Then I recreated my social media presence with a non-business IG account geared to be of real service to others sharing empowering messages and eventually promoting this book. Frankly, I don't care about the "follow" count here; if you like the message, "follow," if not, then don't. It's all part of a grander plan to enjoy the freedom of being an Authentic.

Be aware that most people just "like" or "follow" so they can increase their own profile numbers. We don't need validation from people we know and most certainly not from people we don't know. It's an exhausting battle to keep up false images. Our self-esteem is created by our own mindset; the choices we make and the actions that follow. No one's opinion of you is more important than your own. So, I'm going to say it again: Ditch the social media as you start on your journey to becoming an Authentic.

Too harsh you say? Then try to be judicious in how much time you allot to interacting with any of the sites. Much like any addiction, you'll go through withdrawal, but over time you'll wonder why you devoted so much time to such an ego-driven activity. (Remember: Authentics learn to leave their egos at the door and have a healthy grasp on their self-esteem at the exclusion of other's opinions). Trust me, your days will become filled with more meaningful, soul-satisfying activities that will add to a foundation necessary to have a more authentic life.

Taking Inventory

Now let's talk about creating that foundation for your authentic journey. Remember in the last chapter I discussed assessing your authentic qualities, or lack of, and I encouraged you to be brutal as you assessed yourself. Now it's time to write them down.

Use a blank piece of paper for this. Draw a vertical line down the center, and on one half write down the things you're fond of about yourself. On the other half write what you're not fond of about yourself. I have found that putting these assessments in writing instills a reality check in the writer; when you're looking at your lists, it's hard to run or hide. Our goodness as well as our faults stare at us in black and white, and there's a subconscious shift in our psyche that we're committed to follow through

Try to look at your "not fond of" list without judgment. We all have faults and make mistakes. Depending on the fault, here is an opportunity to reduce your list to as few things as possible. However, be realistic when deciding which "fault" needs attention. Only the ones that impact others negatively and that you can control deserve priority. This exercise is about character, not physical, issues. Be grateful and humble for your "fond" list because it shows that along the way, you've made some good choices that have made you who you are in the present moment. Don't be fooled about the bad choices, though; they're actually more important than the good ones because those are opportunities that help us to grow. By being challenged we must dig deep to overcome the struggle and in doing so, we grow. Growth equals happiness and joy, and isn't that why we are ultimately here on this planet? To be joyful is a gift—our right!—but it comes at a price and that's where the work comes in.

Below your two lists, write down a mantra (affirmation) that sums up all that you want to achieve. Keep it simple, one or two lines at the most, as it will become your daily mantra, sun up and sun down. For example, mine is, "Today is a *great* day! Thank you for all that I am and all that I'll ever be. I humbly ask for your continued guidance in making daily choices that keep me on my authentic path."

I always like to give gratitude before I ask for anything. I believe the Universe doesn't like a constant taker who never expresses gratitude. Create your mantra that you believe with all your heart so that saying it daily will become ingrained in your psyche. Write it down and find a place to post in your home so that it's the first thing you see in the morning and the last thing you see at night. Recite it throughout the day or in any situation where you feel yourself making a choice not in alignment with your authenticity goal.

Choices

Speaking of choices; life is always a series of choices. The choices we've made throughout our lives are responsible for making us who we are. We know when a choice is not right— that feeling we get in our gut is the red flag that something is not quite right. People tend to ignore that gut feeling ,but I'm here to tell you that when you do, you'll usually wish that you had paid attention to it. I know from my own life experiences that when I ignore my gut feelings about something or someone, there's always something I need to go back and clean up. Training ourselves to listen to our gut feelings is a *huge* step towards living more authentically. An Authentic knows that life will throw them those curve balls—life lessons—and the key is to acknowledge, accept, reflect, and learn. No one is immune but it's *how* we handle the chaos around us that defines us, not the chaos itself.

Good Morning, Good Morning

Here are a few other tools you can use as you embark on this journey to being an Authentic. Ask yourself before your feet hit the floor, "Who will I meet today that will change my life?" Better yet, whose life will *you* change? The change doesn't have to be grandiose; the simplest of acts can change someone's life in an instant. A random act of kindness, a sincere compliment, a phone call to just see how someone is doing are some of the ways to change and be changed.

A Gratitude List

Create a Gratitude List. Write down what you're grateful for and don't be stingy. Be thankful for your health, your significant other, for having a roof over your head, food in your pantry, friends and family that love you, and for the gift of *Life*! Thank your organs for working properly, thank the Universe for knowing when to give you what you need when you need it. Conversely, thank the Universe for removing toxic things or people from your life because you didn't need it or them. Thank the simplest of things or the grandest of things. We all have a lot more to be thankful for than we realize when we open our eyes to the hardships of others. Be grateful for the smallest of things!

When you've completed your list, recite or read it first thing in the morning and last thing at night. This helps to keep life's events in perspective when the "pity monster" comes to visit.

Remember, your attitude determines your aptitude. See your challenges as opportunities for growth that can reveal another layer of your authentic self. Feed your mind daily with inspirational material; indulge liberally and often to feed your soul and keep it filled. When you're faced with a situation and not clear about a solution, ask yourself, "What would the *real* me do?"

Actions Create Habits

Becoming an Authentic is like training for a marathon event. Create daily habits that build the mind, body, and soul that include exercise, meditation, and eating well. Read anything you can get your hands on that reinforces the information I've shared. At the end of this book is a partial list of some of the resources I've used in my own authenticity training. Start your own list as well. Who and what inspires you? Perhaps you'll make this book one of them. Listen to others' perspectives and stories on the subject, stay in the present moment as much as possible, and forgive yourself when you stray from your path. To become an Authentic in a world of fakes, one must be audacious and not everyone has the courage to do this. There will be people and situations that try to distract you from your authentic path, but once you build your foundation of integrity and experience the amount of true joy you're creating, their importance and influence in your life will fade away. Your goal is to surround yourself with people who encourage, inspire, and set a higher standard for you to be better.

Living life on your own terms is an exhilarating place to be but it's available only to those who work to achieve it. I don't know about you, but I certainly don't want to be on my death bed saying "if only..." because I was too afraid to be *me*. It will be too late then. ~

FOOD for THOUGHT:
You only have 48 hours to live.
What will matter the most to you?

BEING AN AUTHENTIC TO BENEFIT OTHERS

Leading by Example

Let others see their own greatness when looking in your eyes.

~ Mollie Marti

UP TO NOW, WE HAVE:

- defined authenticity,
- learned why it's so important to be an Authentic,
- recognized the traits of an Authentic,
- discovered how to find it in ourselves and others.

Let's explore how you being You can benefit others.

An Authentic has the courage and boldness to stand in their own truth. When one has that kind of courage of conviction, it shows tremendous responsibility and trust that they possess to share their vulnerable, genuine self to others. The response from others is usually positive and in turn, if they're paying attention, can give them the impetus to step up to their own authentic personalities without fear of repercussion. Being around an authentic person can be contagious in so many positive ways that one can't help but "answer the call" to authenticity. An Authentic doesn't have their attention on being judged. This is huge in the life-affirming stage for anyone. Again, think of this as removing a plastic bag off one's head—*now* you can breathe and be! Imagine the ripple of positive change in the world that can come from people standing in their own integrity, awareness and truth! Imagine less pretentiousness, less fakery, less fear, less dishonesty, less anger. One can quickly see how the joy of authenticity brought to the surface and shared with others in a loving and positive way could impact our world. How could anyone say no to that?

As you move forward on your journey, pay attention to the types of people who become drawn to you. Are they authentic and empowered like you, contributing positive energy? Or are they needy, broken and energy draining? Are they jealous of your authenticity and doing subtle things to sabotage your efforts?

"We attract what we are." If you're committed to your authentic path, then anyone bringing less to your journey has no room in your life. If they're already in your life, let them go. If they're trying to enter, refuse to accept their presence. This is your life and there can be no guilt or feeling selfish about saying a big, fat *No!* to anyone not valuing your authenticity. Not everyone will get it and that's not on you but on them.

The Serenity Prayer, which is the mantra of the AA community, is spot on for every one of us on any day we are walking this planet: "Grant me the serenity to accept what I cannot change (that would be others and all that goes on around me); the courage to change the things I can (that would be *me* and my response to others and everything going on around me); and the wisdom to know the difference." Say it daily, or whenever you need confirmation that you are on the right path. Being an Authentic takes daily work and once you commit to it, the choices you make will become a lot easier to make, I promise.

I wish you so much success on your journey! Life is here for the taking so go out take the *biggest* bites you want, go even *farther* out on that limb, and don't look back unless you want to go that way – your future is so bright! ~

FOOD for THOUGHT
Who has inspired you with the life they are living?

AUTHENTICITY UNCORKED
"meraki"

Meraki [may-rah'-kee] (adjective) from Greek. This is a word that modern Greeks often use to describe doing something with soul, creativity, or love—when you put something of yourself into what you're doing, whatever it may be.

WANT TO LEAVE YOU WITH THIS word because it is so closely aligned with what being an Authentic is about. I came across it in one of my usual "putzing" periods on the computer. I love studying the English language, the origins and definitions of various words intrigues the heck out of me. So up pops this word and when I saw what it meant I *knew* I had found a word that described me to a T.

When starting my catering business, I did extensive research on what it would be called. It was very important that the name represented my values, beliefs, and the essence of what my business would offer. I chose Alma because *alma* is Spanish for "soul," and that's who I am; that's what feeding people is about for me— feeding their soul, not just a hole. Over the years, I've received tons of positive feedback, not only about the name but our service as a catering company. I've instilled that same kind of "soul" spirit in the people who work for me—no shortcuts or half-assing anything when taking care of our clients. That comes across in our service and is reflected in the feedback we constantly receive from our clientele.

Had I found *meraki* earlier, I would have named my business Meraki. Rather than lose the word from my life, I hired a letter artist to create the word in 12-inch letters in a special font to hang in my house. I love this word so much that I wanted to see it every day as a reminder of my daily purpose—more food for my soul (no pun intended). Then I chose a series of words to be placed underneath in smaller font that represented that Meraki Mindset™—*authenticity*, of course! (The others were passion, soul, gratitude, patience, curiosity, abundance, and wisdom.) Now I can look at them daily as part of my mantras and meditations. I am all for any way I can feed my soul positively and on a regular basis.

I encourage you to find your own "meraki" and apply it to *everything* you pursue, no matter how big or small. Kisses and best wishes to you on your authentic journey. May it be as grand as you are! ~

FOOD for THOUGHT:
Where in your life will you add the element of *meraki*?

_____

_____

_____

_____

_____

_____

_____

_____

_____

_____

_____

_____

_____

_____

_____

_____

_____

_____

_____

_____

THE MANDALAS

THROUGHOUT THIS BOOK YOU HAVE SEEN a variety of mandalas (pronounced "muhn-DA-luh"). Their placement is most definitely intentional as I want to help you with your journey to achieving becoming an Authentic.

Mandalas were created in the service of Buddhism. They were originally produced in Asia. Now they are produced throughout the world.

Mandalas are designed to balance their visual elements, symbolizing unity and harmony. The meanings of a mandala depend on color, geometric elements, and culture. The purpose of the mandala is to serve as a tool on our spiritual journey as it symbolizes cosmic and psychic order and as an aid to meditation. Many cultures have used mandalas.

The colors in a mandala hold great significance:

RED
Strength, high energy and passion

PINK
Love, intuition, and the feminine

ORANGE
Creativity, transformation, self-awareness,and intuition

YELLOW
Learning, wisdom, laughter, and happiness

GREEN
Physical healing, psychic ability, love of nature and caring

On page 39 I have included several mandalas for you to color. Think about the color meanings and grab yourself a set of crayons, markers or colored pencils. Allow your personality to show as you color and don't be afraid to let your "inner child" fly (when is the last time you colored anything?) There is no right or wrong way to color; this is a personal exercise and an expression of you and where you are in your immediate space and time. Take your time as you go through this exercise; they don't all have to be done at once. In fact, you might notice that your color choices and place-ment of them will be vastly different depending on your mindset.

Think about framing them or just hanging them around your house. To keep the natural flow of energy going throughout your house, consider the bedroom, bathroom, or near the front door. Hanging your mandalas on the wall can serve as protection from negative energy and unwelcome emotions of anger, hatred, or depression. May you experience perpetual unity and harmony. ~

MANTRAS

THE FOLLOWING ARE SOME OF THE mantras alluded to in this book and that have served me well on my authenticity journey. I keep most next to my bed and read one or more a night, depending on my mindset, before I turn off the light. The last activity you're involved in before you fall asleep is the one that is imprinted on your brain for the night—subliminal suggestion, if you will. My list is ever evolving as I'm constantly in search of "soul food" to keep me on point.

"We don't get what we want out of life,
we get what we are."
~ adapted from Les Brown

"Enjoy the present smiling moment."
~ adapted from Thích Nhất Hạnh

"It's not what happens to us or around us,
but what happens within us that defines us."
~ adapted from Elizabeth Smart

"I trust this process of Life to show me my highest good
through positive experiences."
~ adapted from Louis Hay

"Action is magic."
~ adapted from Goethe

"No one can make you feel a certain way
without your permission."
~ adapted from Eleanor Roosevelt

"It is only with the heart that one can see rightly,
for what is essential is invisible to the eye."
~ Antoine de Saint-Exupéry

"Your attitude determines your aptitude."
~ adapted from Zig Ziegler

"I will not die an unlived life
because one day this will all be over."
~ adapted from Dawna Markova & Michael Josephson

"How will you use this one Wild and Precious Life?"
~ adapted from Mary Oliver

"The minute we are born, we begin to die;
therefore, our sole goal is to find out our life's purpose,
as soon as possible, and get on with the job of *living*."
~ adapted from Janne Teller

31

KICK-ASS ACCOUNTABILIITY

Will the Real You Please Stand Up?

You're at the point where the rubber meets the road. We've discussed the concept of becoming an Authentic and if you've digested the information here, you know that "nothin' comes from nothin'." The reflections and notes you've created have all come from your sincere desire to become the most authentic person you can be. That means vulnerability, honesty, and accountability were foremost in the answers revealed to you on your journey. Remember, you are only accountable to *you*. At the end of the day when everyone else has fallen by the wayside, the only person you'll be left with is *you*. So be good to yourself and stay accountable. ~

Take notes on these pages, from this book or from other resources you come across, that support your authentic goals.

Using the meaning of mandala colors I've described on page 29, color these mandalas to support you as you begin your journey and as an expression of your authentic self.

"Gut feelings are my Guardian Angels."

"Attract what you want by being what you want."

"Life is all about choices;
change yours and you change your life."

"Today I'm taking bigger bites."

"Thank you for all that I am
and all that I'll ever be."

RESOURCES

BOOKS

Reflections on Life:
Why We're Here and How to Enjoy the Journey
by Allen Klein

The Seat of the Soul
by Gary Zukav

A Thousand Paths to Wisdom
by David Baird

365 Inspirations: Self & Spirit
by Duncan Baird Publishers

On Becoming Fearless…in Love, Work, and Life
by Arianna Huffington

POETRY

"What Will Matter"
by Michael Josephson

"I Will Not Die an Unlived Life"
by Dawna Markova

ACKNOWLEDGMENTS

I WAS RECENTLY ASKED HOW I CAME to know how to write a book with no prior experience. That question came from someone afraid to take a chance on most things. What they don't know is that I've learned through a lot of living that playing it safe makes one a very dull person. Dull and me are rarely in the same sentence, or so I'm told by my husband and friends. My life is about being as authentic as possible on a daily basis and in order to do that, there needs to be challenges. Challenges equal growth, growth equals true joy, and my sole goal is to stay on my path of joy.

I realize that no man is an island, no matter how independent or self-made they think they are. To that end, I need to acknowledge those who have made me who I am as I write this.

My parents—I want to thank my parents who gave me life and raised me with a foundation of discipline, honesty, integrity, hard

45

work, gratitude, and humility. I watched them sacrifice plenty to provide for seven kids and yet we never felt deprived or lacking of wants and necessities. They also didn't believe in sparing the rod and while I hated it then, I sure get the why now, and look at me—I turned out okay.

My siblings would warrant a thank you for helping to shape me, especially when we're at odds. I say "especially" because those are the times when one is tested in any relationship, but the blood ones test you the most. Life is too short for grudges so we try to keep it real and honor our legacy.

My teachers throughout my years of education inspired me to be the best student possible due to their belief and encouragement in my potential.

Anne Dodson, my BFF from my grade-school years, is so much like family that we laugh to this day about how much time we spent at each other's houses. She is my sounding board when I need to get some insight about sibling issues or some stupidity in life. Anne is my "sista from another mista."

My education—I'm grateful for my experience with higher education where being exposed to a variety of mindsets and perspectives helped me form some of my most critical thinking. My parents' insistence that I get a diploma was so elemental in my development that I ended up getting two.

The U. S. military—I would be remiss not sending gratitude to the U. S. military. When I reflect on my time spent as a soldier, I know that no other experience that I've gone through in my life has shaped me more. The challenges I endured as a minority female in "this man's Army" give new meaning to the term "growth." Here's how you know you've grown—when you've beaten the odds and can say after the fact that you wouldn't do it again but are grateful for the life lessons. That's some powerful stuff there!

My husband deserves some of my most sincere acknowledgment. He has been instrumental in showing me what being authentic truly looks like without even really trying (but don't tell him that!). Authenticity just seems to come naturally to him and I believe it stems from having the courage of his convictions. He is an extremely intelligent, thought-provoking individual who's perfectly content with the simple means of life. Funny as hell too with a penchant for telling the most Lucille Ball-like stories—never a dull moment with him as most of our friends can attest. I tell him often how grateful I am for him having my back all these years, unconditionally and always with the utmost sincere intentions.

My circle of friends—Let me acknowledge the relationships I have with my tight friends circle. The circle is intentionally small as I have found over the years that many use that word "friend" way too loosely, in my humble opinion. I hate titles and pretense, but my friends are given this title because of the truths we speak, together or apart. We have a spoken rule to hold each other's feet to the fire no matter what, but in a loving, supportive, respectful way. And when it gets too hot in the kitchen, we have the grace and humility to patch things up because that's how important we are in each other's lives.

Being a business owner in our community has afforded me many opportunities to meet all kinds of people. There are some that deserve acknowledgment by name because of their influence on my personal/business growth and in no particular order. Please indulge me and I pray I haven't left out anyone:

Ib Hamide, restaurant owner and product entrepreneur, has always unselfishly given me his time, friendship, and advice. I can always count on his guidance and wisdom to give me direction and help me make those tough calls that are sometimes necessary in this wild ride called Life. He's as authentic as they come.

Cedric Rudd, my "brotha from another motha" from day one, showed me who he was with the world's greatest smile. We've had some really "let your hair down" conversations and know that we've always got each other's back. I'm always teasing him about giving the greatest hugs.

Annemieke Golly used to be my personal training client and loves to regale others about our first time meeting. She claims I was intimidating (who, me?) and trained her like a drill sergeant (probably my military background creeping in just a bit lol). She survived and thrived, and to this day we are tight friends who laugh about life and its absurdities and always express our gratitude for our abundances and our friendship. I admire her physical, spiritual, and mental strength—she seems to never let anything become an obstacle to achieving her goals.

Jill Sager was my drum teacher years ago. We didn't really form a friendship until long after those classes ended but we have some deep chats about Life. I love how she's opened my eyes to her culture and passion for spiritual growth. Her jugular style of input with that East Coast edge matches mine so much that we laugh about the blood we'd leave if we used weapons other than our tongues. She's such a hoot!

Sandi Thompson also doesn't pull any punches and is another good friend. She and I share an intense passion for really good food, wine, and travel.

Darby Giannone and Marvin Révoal, business owners in our community, are some of the smartest, strongest people I know. Darby is small in stature but oh, what a mighty force! Her wisdom and guidance are much appreciated. Marvin has always been generous with his wisdom and insights as well. I highly respect their integrity, achievements, and humility.

My man Benj Upstein and I have only been friends for a short time but hit it off immediately. We share so much of the same spiritual, mental, and social energy that I swear we were twins at birth. Benj is so passionate about life and everything in it that sometimes it seems he's going to burst from the inside because his body can't hold it all. I love his passion and his East Coast way of putting it all on the line. He, too, has opened my eyes to his culture and his commitment to making the world a better place.

Rose Bessman is my good friend from the health club days. She is like family and is as generous with her possessions as she is with her wisdom.

Esther Celis and Ulrich Richter are my international infusions of culture in our social circle. Esther is another small but mighty force in a very quiet, humble, graceful way. She has such a way of turning the simplest ingredients into the most amazing dishes! I've learned a lot watching her work her magic in the kitchen. She has her hands full with running the family business and keeping Ulrich in line! He's my crazy German who I can always count on to bring so much life to any occasion. He's quite the raconteur and scholar too. Love them both.

This book would not be possible without two very significant women: **Val Stilwell and Eva Long**. Val and I have worked together before; she was instrumental in creating the brand image for my catering business and the dry rubs line I'd created a few years ago. Her expertise and skill sets have garnered me plenty of praise on the eye-catching, professional look of my catering website, marketing materials, and packaging for my dry rub line. Val has the energy of ten people! That might be conservative lol but she is always "on." Her mind is in a constant state of creating and reflecting and producing. She wears me out sometimes just hearing her schedule, but she just keeps going. And talk about handy! If she doesn't know how to do something, anything, you can best believe she will figure it out or die trying. Collaborating with her on this book, she supplied all of the mandalas and decora you see, contributed some of the editing, and created the concepts for the front and back covers. It felt like old home week. We know each other very well from a personality and work ethics viewpoint and I knew that this endeavor would be in great hands with her on board. Phenomenal mind and strong woman—two of my favorite traits. Eva Long came to me as a referral from Val who highly encouraged me to get to know her. The two of them have collaborated on many other books so they know each other's style really well. Another strong woman with a super creative eye. Eva played the chief editor on this book and after each edit and rewrite, I learned so much from her about composition and intentional messaging. She has been tough but gentle with her feedback; when we had a difference of opinion about something, we'd each pitch our case. Sometimes she won; sometimes she didn't, but there was always respect and no ego. Our mutual goal was, and is, to put out the very best product possible. I know that my project is in great hands with Eva; she's my editing/publishing "mother," gently but expertly guiding me through the whole process. I look forward to more collaborations with both women.

If I've forgotten anyone on this list, *mea culpa* a thousand times. I consider those who have broken bread with me or have stepped into my private domain as my friends on every different level. You know who you are. ~

ROBIN-BROWN-WOOD has spent her life transforming herself in search of her authentic path. She grew up an Army brat, moving around the South with her family, who eventually settled in the Midwest. Her job choices are as varied as her addresses: a variety of sale positions, librarian, landscaper, freelance photographer, various positions in food and beverage, personal trainer, clothing designer, combat Veteran. She holds two degrees and has served on the boards and committees of a variety of local non-profits whose missions fuel her passion for giving back to her community.

Currently, she owns Alma Catering, a full-service catering company that feeds five to five hundred people at a variety of events throughout Lane County, Oregon. She lives in Eugene, Oregon, with her husband.

For more empowering and audacious messages, follow Robin's IG profile "thepath.less.followed" and her Li'l Liva Publishing page on FB. You can check out her website where additional copies of *Audacious Authenticity* in both print and eBook can be purchased.

lillivapublishing.com

Made in the USA
Middletown, DE
08 August 2021